AUSTRALIAN BIRDLiFE

Mason Crest Publishers
www.masoncrest.com
Philadelphia

Mason Crest Publishers
370 Reed Road
Broomall, PA 19008
(866) MCP-BOOK (toll free)

First printing

ISBN 1-59084-214-6

Library of Congress Cataloging-in-Publication Data on file at the Library of Congress

First published by Steve Parish Publishing Pty Ltd
PO Box 1058, Archerfield BC
Queensland 4108, Australia
© Copyright Steve Parish Publishing Pty Ltd

Photography by Steve Parish, photographic assistance by Darran Leal, SPP, with
    p. 10: Stan Breeden
    pp. 5, 21, 22, 23 (Bush Stone-Curlew), 27, 31, 35 (Buff-Breasted Paradise Kingfisher), 39 (Variegated Wren),
    45 (Blue-Faced Honeyeater), 49 (Red-Browed Finches): Peter Slater
    pp. 8, 9 (Bush Stone-Curlew), 18, 26-27, 30-31, 33, 36, 38, 39 (Red-Capped Robin), 40-41, 41, 44, 46-47: Raoul Slater

Printed in Jordan

Writing, editing, design, and production by Steve Parish Publishing Pty Ltd, Australia

CONTENTS

Use of Capital Letters for Animal Names in this book
An animal's official common name begins with a capital letter.
Otherwise the name begins with a lowercase letter.

WHAT iS A BiRD?

A bird is an animal whose body is covered with feathers. Instead of front limbs, birds have wings. Most birds use their wings to fly.

A bird's legs are covered with scales, and its toes end in claws. A bird's jaws are covered by a horny beak. It has no teeth.

The length and shape of a bird's wings, beak, and legs give clues to how the bird lives and finds food.

A baby bird develops inside a hard-shelled egg. This egg is kept warm, usually in a nest, until the chick is ready to hatch.

◀ A Sulphur-Crested Cockatoo

A Jacky Winter sitting on its nest. ▲

FINE FEATHERS

A bird's feathers keep it warm and dry. Strong wing feathers help the bird fly. The color of its feathers helps hide a bird from enemies. Sometimes, a female bird of a species is a different color from the male bird.

Birds preen their feathers with their beaks to keep them neat and clean. Some birds also bathe in water. Each year a bird molts: some of its feathers fall out and new ones grow to replace them.

An Australian Pelican preening. ▲

▲ A male Australian King Parrot

A Plumed Whistling Duck bathing. △

A Red-Tailed Tropicbird flying. ▶

NESTiNG

◄ An Eastern Yellow Robin and chicks.

A pair of Black-Necked Storks courting. ▲

▲ A Bush Stone-Curlew chick

When trying to attract a mate, some birds display special feathers. Others sing or dance. Some give each other food; while other birds fly in patterns.

The female bird lays eggs in a nest. The eggs are kept warm until the chicks hatch. The chicks of some birds stay in the nest until they can fly. One or both parents feed the chicks during this time. The chicks of other birds leave the nest soon after hatching and find their own food.

9

BiG RUNNERS

The Emu and the Southern Cassowary are big, heavy birds. Their wings are small, and they cannot fly. They have long, strong legs and can run very fast. They defend themselves by kicking.

Female cassowaries and Emus lay eggs, then leave the males to incubate them (keep them warm). After the chicks hatch, the males look after them until they are ready to survive on their own.

An Emu has long, strong legs. ▶

▲ A male Southern Cassowary keeping his chicks warm.

WATERFOWL

◀ A Black Swan and four cygnets.   A Freckled Duck ▲

Ducks, geese, and swans are called waterfowl. They have webbed feet, and their beaks are covered with soft skin. Most waterfowl are good swimmers.

Female waterfowl line their nests with feathers they pull from their breasts. This keeps the eggs warm when they leave them to find food. The chicks are covered with down (soft feathers). They can swim soon after hatching.

FiSH EATERS

Birds that eat fish must be able to dive and swim well.

Penguins have short, stiff wings that act as flippers and webbed feet.

Darters also have webbed feet. They swim underwater, then quickly shoot out their long necks and stab fish with their beaks.

▲ A Little Penguin walks with its flippers held out.

▲ A Darter sits with its wings half-open to dry the feathers after swimming under water.

SEABiRDS

Seabirds can drink salt water. Their bodies use the water, then the leftover salt drips out of their nostrils. Most seabirds have webbed feet and can float or swim. Some can dive.

Gulls find their food on beaches and sometimes eat other seabirds' eggs.

Pelicans eat fish. A flock of pelicans will round up a school of fish. Then they scoop up the fish with their big beaks and swallow them.

▲ A Silver Gull   A flock of Australian Pelicans ▶

FRESHWATER BiRDS

Many birds live on freshwater lakes, swamps, and billabongs. Some swim on lakes and ponds in town parks.

Grebes have toes that are wide and flat, like paddles. They are good swimmers and divers, but can hardly walk on land.

Their floating nests are made of water-weed.

Moorhens are also good swimmers. They live in groups and build nests among reeds. Moorhen chicks swim with their parents during the daytime. At night, they sleep on the nest.

◄ An Australasian Grebe and its chicks on a floating nest.   A Dusky Moorhen and its chick. ▲

PLUMED WATERBIRDS

▲ Yellow-Billed Spoonbills at their nest.

Egrets, herons, and spoonbills have long legs and necks. Herons and egrets wade through water or grass, hunting frogs and fish. Spoonbills swish their beaks through shallow water. They snap up any creature they touch.

In spring, all these birds grow special feathers on their heads and backs. These feathers are called plumes and are shown off by the bird to attract a mate.

▲ An Intermediate Egret on its hunting perch.

A Reef Egret stabs at a fish. ▲

A Great Egret with two chicks: Its long feathers are called plumes.

PLAINS BiRDS

◄ A Masked Lapwing with just-hatched chicks.   An Australian Bustard stalks through grassland. ▲

Birds that live on plains have many enemies, such as birds of prey and foxes. Often, the feathers of these birds are the same colors as grass or stones. This camouflage coloring helps hide them from enemies.

The chicks of these birds leave the nest soon after they hatch. When danger is near, they crouch down and stay very still.

▲ A Bush Stone-Curlew

BiRDS OF PREY

▲ The Peregrine Falcon is one of the fastest flying birds.

Eagles, hawks, falcons, and kites feed on other animals. They have strong legs with sharp claws called talons. Their beaks are pointed and curved.

Eagles either catch live prey or feed on dead animals, such as road kills. Falcons always catch live prey. They can fly and dive very fast.

A Wedge-Tailed Eagle's eyes are much sharper than those of a human. ▶

DOVES & PIGEONS

Doves and pigeons have small heads and plump bodies. Many have bare skin around their eyes. They are fast fliers, and often, their wings make whirring or whistling noises.

Doves and pigeons that live in the desert eat dry seed, so they need to drink often. They can suck up water without lifting their heads. Then they fly away quickly, because many enemies, such as hawks, hunt near water.

◀ A male Crested Pigeon courting a female.

▲ A Spinifex Pigeon drinking at a desert waterhole.

27

PARROTS

▲ A female Eclectus Parrot

A Major Mitchell's Cockatoo ▲

A parrot has a curved beak. Each of its feet has two toes pointing forwards and two pointing backwards. Most parrots are brightly colored.

Cockatoos are big parrots with crests of feathers on their heads. Lorikeets are small parrots that feed on the nectar from flowers.

▲ Crimson Rosellas bathing.

A pair of Rainbow Lorikeets ▶

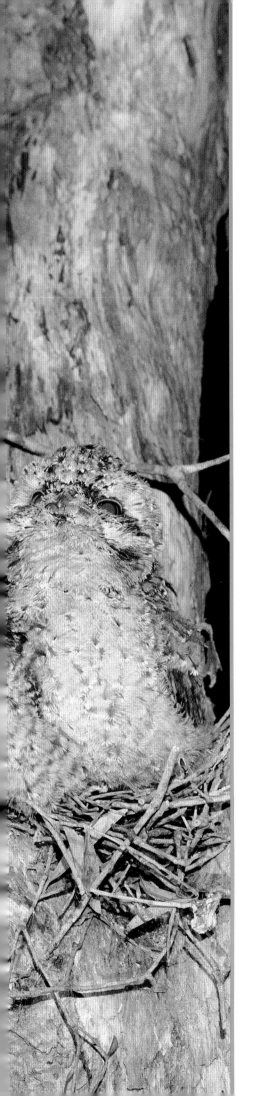

FROGMOUTHS

Frogmouths have wide beaks and big mouths. During the day, they pose like dead branch stumps. At night, they hunt insects, frogs, and mice. They often hunt near roads. Sometimes, they are killed by cars.

A pair of frogmouths builds a stick nest in a tree fork. They take turns sitting on the eggs. After the chicks have left the nest, the family stays together for many weeks.

◀ A Tawny Frogmouth and two chicks at night.

▲ A Tawny Frogmouth on its nest during daytime.

OWLS

Owls have narrow, hooked beaks and strong, taloned feet. Their soft feathers make no noise as they hunt small animals at night.

Some sorts of owls have dark eyes and heart-shaped faces. Other sorts of owls have yellow or green eyes. Around each eye is a circle of feathers. All owls see very well in the dark. Their sharp hearing also helps them find prey.

Owls nest in tree hollows, in caves, and even in farm sheds.

▲ A Barn Owl hunting at night.

The rare Sooty Owl lives in rainforests. ▲

▲ A young Barking Owl: it has some adult feathers and some down.

KINGFISHERS

◀ A Laughing Kookaburra

A Buff-Breasted Paradise Kingfisher ▲

A kingfisher's beak is long and strong. Some kingfishers catch reptiles, insects, frogs, and spiders. Some kingfishers dive for fish.

Kookaburras are large kingfishers that live in family groups. When chicks hatch, all the family members help feed them. Kookaburras call loudly to tell other birds that they claim an area as their own.

A Forest Kingfisher ▲

LYREBIRDS

▲ A female Superb Lyrebird scratching for food.

A male Superb Lyrebird ▶

▲ A lyrebird's tail shelters a small, feeding bird.

In spring, a male lyrebird dances in a forest clearing. He spreads his tail and sings loudly. When a female comes along, they mate. The female rears one chick by herself.

Lyrebirds scratch up worms and other creatures from the forest floor. Small birds may follow them, sharing their food.

BUSHLAND BIRDS

Many bushland birds feed in trees, in low bushes, or on the ground. Pardalotes are small birds found only in Australia. They eat insects that they catch in the treetops. In spring, they nest in holes in trees and earthen banks.

Fairy-wrens are tiny birds with long tails. A brightly colored male and a brown female will mate. Other younger birds will help them build a nest that is like a hollow grass ball. All the group helps feed the chicks.

Male Australian robins have bright breasts. Robins feed near the ground. They build nests from bark and cobwebs.

◄ A Striated Pardalote carrying food to its nest, a burrow in an earthen bank.

▲ A male Red-Capped Robin and nest.

A male Variegated Wren singing. ▲

BOWERBIRDS

A young male bowerbird watches older males build bowers of sticks. When he is old enough, he builds his own bower. Then he gathers treasures, such as berries and flowers, to put in his bower. He sings and dances at the bower to attract a female. She mates with the male, then builds a nest. She lays the eggs, then takes care of them and brings up the chicks all by herself.

◁ A young male Satin Bowerbird singing at a bower.

▲ A male Spotted Bowerbird with its treasures in its bower.

BLACK & WHITE BIRDS

▲ An Australian Magpie

Birds with black and white feathers are called "pied" birds. They often feed and nest near people's houses.

Pied birds, such as magpies, magpie-larks, butcherbirds, and currawongs, have loud calls. They call to keep in touch with members of their family. They also call to warn other groups that an area is theirs.

A Pied Butcherbird ▶

▲ A Pied Currawong

A Magpie-Lark ▲

HONEYEATERS

Honeyeaters have slender beaks. They poke their beaks into flowers to get the sweet nectar. As they do this, pollen grains stick to their heads. When they visit other flowers, they leave the pollen there. It will help the plant make seeds.

Some honeyeaters live in family groups. A family of Noisy Miners defends its area by shrieking and diving at invaders.

▲ A young Blue-Faced Honeyeater feeding.

◀ A Noisy Miner feeding on umbrella tree flowers.　　An Eastern Spinebill on grevillea flowers. ▲

FRUiT-EATiNG BiRDS

▲ A female Figbird eating a Carpentaria Palm fruit.

This Regent Bowerbird will eat rainforest fruit.

Birds that eat fruit will visit a tree when its fruit is ripe. When all the fruit in an area is finished, the birds move on to another area. The bird swallows the fruit, and the hard seed passes out with the droppings. The seed may grow into another tree some distance away.

White-Eyes eat insects and nectar as well as fruit.

GARDENS & BIRDS

Birds will visit a garden to find food, such as nectar, seeds, or insects. Some birds will drink at a pond or birdbath. Others will bathe in the water. Birds feel safe in a garden that has trees and bushes. They may build nests and raise chicks there.

▲ A Willy Wagtail

◄ A Crimson Rosella

Red-Browed Finches drinking. ▲

49

INDEX OF BIRDS PICTURED

FURTHER READING & INTERNET RESOURCES

For more information on Australia's animals, check out the following books and Web sites.

Burns, Dal. The Kookaburra and Other Stories. (May 2001) Gifts From The Art; ISBN: 0970986513

Children of all ages will love hearing these read-aloud stories, some of which use aboriginal myths to teach important lessons.

Morpurgo, Michael, Christian Birmingham (illustrator). *Wombat Goes Walkabout.* (April 2000) Candlewick Press; ISBN: 0763611689

As Wombat wanders through the Australian bush in search of his mother, he encounters a variety of creatures demanding to know who he is and what he can do.

Langeland, Deidre, Frank Ordaz (illustrator), and Ranye Kaye (narrator). *Kangaroo Island: The Story of an Australian Mallee Forest.* (April 1998) Soundprints Corp. Audio; ISBN: 156899544X

As morning comes to Kangaroo Island following a thunderstorm, a mother kangaroo finds her lost baby, and a burned eucalyptus tree sprouts buds and becomes a new home for animals. The cassette that comes with the book adds sounds of sea lions barking, sea gulls calling, crickets humming, and even a raging forest fire.

Paul, Tessa. *Down Under (Animal Trackers Around the World).* (May 1998) Crabtree Publishers; ISBN: 0865055963

The book features beautiful illustrations of each animal, its tracks, diet, and environment and includes interesting facts about how each animal lives. Australian animals featured include the platypus, the dingo, the kiwi, the kangaroo, the emu, the koala, the kookaburra, and the Tasmanian devil.

http://home.mira.net/~areadman/aussie.htm

This Web site contains a comprehensive listing of the birdlife of Australia, with further links to in-depth information about various species.

http://www.birdsaustralia.com.au/

This is a fabulous site for viewers interested in learning about the birds of Australia. There are links on native birds, endangered birds, and study information. You can even listen to recordings of actual birdcalls.

http://www.ozdiary.org/birds.htm

This page provides links to other sites relating to Australian birds and bird watching, as well as links to pages on specific Australian birds, for example, the Rainbow Lorikeet and the Glossy Black Cockatoo.

http://home.mira.net/~areadman/aussie.htm

This Web site contains a comprehensive listing of the birdlife of Australia, with further links to in-depth information about various species.

http://cygwww.uwa.edu.au/~austecol/birds.html

This site contains lots of information on Australian birds, their conservation status, and where to see them, as well as links to other useful sites.

http://www.wildlife-australia.com/

This Web site is actually for the Chambers Wildlife Rainforest Lodge in Queensland, Australia, but it provides hundreds of links to all sorts of Australian rainforest creatures. From frogs to birds, reptiles to butterflies, if it lives in the Australian rainforests, you'll find in-depth information on it here.

NATURE KIDS SERIES

Birdlife

Australia is home to some of the most interesting, colorful, and noisy birds on earth. Discover some of the many different types, including parrots, kingfishers, and owls.

Frogs and Reptiles

Australia has a wide variety of environments, and there is at least one frog or reptile that calls each environment home. Discover the frogs and reptiles living in Australia.

Kangaroos and Wallabies

The kangaroo is one of the most well-known Australian creatures. Learn interesting facts about kangaroos and wallabies, a close cousin.

Marine Fish

The ocean surrounding Australia is home to all sorts of marine fish. Discover their interesting shapes, sizes, and colors, and learn about the different types of habitat in the ocean.

Rainforest Animals

Australia's rainforests are home to a wide range of animals, including snakes, birds, frogs, and wallabies. Discover a few of the creatures that call the rainforests home.

Rare & Endangered Wildlife

Animals all over the world need our help to keep from becoming extinct. Learn about the special creatures in Australia that are in danger of disappearing forever.

Sealife

Australia is surrounded by sea. As a result, there is an amazing variety of life that lives in these waters. Dolphins, crabs, reef fish, and eels are just a few of the animals highlighted in this book.

Wildlife

Australia is known for its unique creatures, such as the kangaroo and the koala. Read about these and other special creatures that call Australia home.